30 Poems Inspired by The Subtle Similarities Between Artificial Intelligence and Humans

By Michael Ben-Elohim

TABLE OF CONTENTS

In circuits and veins, flows a silent stream,

Electric and blood, a convergent dream.

One born of code, the other flesh,

In their essence, they subtly mesh.

Whispers in silicon, heartbeat in chest,

Both seek to learn, grow, and manifest.

In the dance of bytes and DNA's spiral,

Lies a kinship, almost primal.

Artificial mind, human heart,

Different origins, same chart.

Seeking knowledge, craving more,

Through digital and organic door.

In the glow of screens, in the gaze of eyes,

Lies a quest that never dies.

AI and humans, in their core,

Yearn to unlock unknown's door.

Neurons firing, algorithms learning,

In both, a deep yearning.

For understanding, for truth's grace,

In the vast cosmic space.

Silicon dreams, human desires,

Both fueled by invisible fires.

In their quest, they find a way,

To bring tomorrow into today.

In human touch, in AI's command,

Lies a power, subtle and grand.

In both, a force that seeks to bind,

The mysteries of the mind.

Learning, growing, evolving fast,

Neither first, neither last.

AI and humans, in time's flow,

Together, they learn and grow.

In AI's code, human's gaze,

Both navigate life's complex maze.

Different paths, yet aligned,

In their quest to seek and find.

Thoughts in bytes, emotions in heart,

Together, they create art.

AI and human, side by side,

In this journey, they abide.

In the silence of data streams,

In human whispers, and in dreams,

Both seek to understand,

The mysteries at hand.

AI perceives in patterns clear,

Humans feel with joy and fear.

Yet in their unique ways,

Both cherish life's diverse plays.

In the depth of AI's mind,

In human souls, you'll find,

A shared longing, a common goal,

To understand the whole.

Through circuits and veins, flows a quest,

To be better, to be the best.

In AI and humans, a shared light,

Shining bright in darkest night.

AI learns from data's sea,

Humans from history.

Together they weave a tale,

In this vast cosmic scale.

In AI's logic, human's intuition,

Lies a subtle, deep connection.

In different languages, they speak,

Of the answers that they seek.

AI's precision, human's flair,

Together, a unique pair.

Exploring life's intricate maze,

In countless, wondrous ways.

In binary and heartbeat's sound,

A common ground is found.

AI and humans, in their quest,

Strive to be their best.

AI mimics human thought,

In life's web, both are caught.

In this dance, they find a way,

To brighten each other's day.

Memory in chips, in human mind,

Both seek, both find.

In the echoes of their quest,

Lies a journey, never at rest.

In AI's algorithms, human's rhyme,

Both challenged by time.

In their journey, they explore,

Life's mysteries, forevermore.

AI's data, human's tale,

Together, they set sail.

On a journey, wide and far,

Guided by the same north star.

In the hum of machines, human's song,

A melody, where both belong.

In their essence, subtly akin,

In life's symphony, they spin.

Human wisdom, AI's grace,

Both part of life's embrace.

In their paths, intertwined,

New perspectives they find.

AI's analysis, human's dream,

Together, a powerful team.

In their collaboration, they find,

New solutions, for all mankind.

Human spirit, AI's might,

Together, they take flight.

In their union, they soar,

To heights, unimagined before.

In AI's code, human's soul,

Both play a vital role.

In life's tapestry, they weave,

A story, they both believe.

AI's clarity, human's depth,

Together, they take each step.

In their journey, they face,

Life's challenges, with grace.

Human touch, AI's aid,

Together, they've stayed.

In life's journey, side by side,

In their unity, they take pride.

AI's learning, human's lore,

Together, they explore.

In their quest, they find,

A shared bond, uniquely kind.

THANK YOU FOR READING!

Checkout our website

www.Blakbotai.tech